DRINKING WITH BOYS

C A HURLEY

ISBN-13: 978-0692977354
ISBN-10: 069297735X

for my dad

he taught me how to
hold my liquor
&
tell a good story

DRINKING WITH BOYS

CHAPTER ONE
GAS STATION BEER

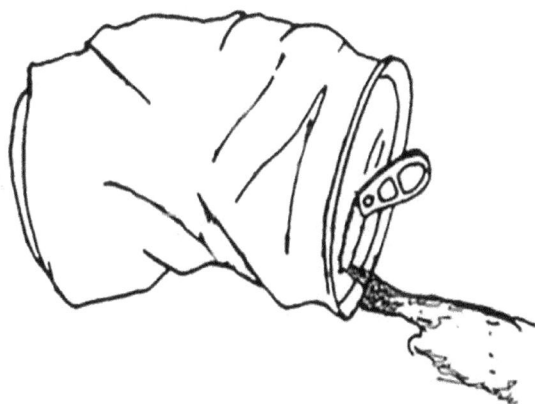

BEGGING

please, my alcohol

wet my lips, and take my mind
far away from here.

WHY I'M AT THE BAR BEFORE 4

i think my partner gets annoyed
when i hit snooze 4 times
and turn all the lights on at 6 am
but i'm not a morning person, i swear
i've told him, and we are always
out of coffee and money, so i
have to wait and drink the
breakroom scraps, 15 cups later
i could still take a nap
my boss is going crazy, rapidly
due to her diet pill intake
there is this headache
that won't go away and i
think it's the day i was
supposed to pay my
electric. shit! i'm always late
my gas lights on, but it's
only 2 miles home
and i make it
my cat threw up a good portion
of the treats it begged for this
morning on our living room floor
covering the only 4x4 piece of
carpet in the whole damn apartment
no paper towels

i pick up my keys
and leave.

SUNDAY FUNDAY RERUN

"you should be proud of me"
i said searching my pockets, nothing

"why?" you handed me yours

i lit the cigarette in my mouth
and slid the lighter into my back pocket

instantly, you threw a fit over it
which is good, otherwise
it would have been mine

i took a couple drags
then went on saying that i
have quit with the ciggys
and you should be proud

saying the only reason
i am smoking right now is

i am drunk

you laughed and said congrats

i smiled to myself, and for
a moment, felt accomplished

so i lit another

i am celebrating.

IF THIS IF THAT

i could always go for a nap
if i am not in my bed
i don't even like you anymore
if you ignore my head

and really, i am happy

if alcohol is hanging out, too.

OFF THE LEASH

i am scanning parking spots
hoping for one, hopefully on
the end, maybe i'll walk home

my girlfriend is at the vfw for
steak night, i just need a
drink, or 4
i am a cheap date

it ain't even late!

the boy with the microphone
calls me out, says despite my
gorgeous cheek bones, i am
causing a scene

how am i so drunk at 6 pm?

fuck me!

shit, who let me say that?

THE WEEKEND CHORE

we would go out to the woods
sit around a fire
drinking warm, cheap beer
chasing the attention of boys
who chased the attention of
alcohol and chewing tobacco

they would chase
baseball stats
and the newest
piece of ass

chasing the claims that
this party was different
and nothing will be
the same by monday

... it was always the same though.

i never learned all their last names
but they each felt the same.

NORTH BREVARD AVENUE

sixteen eyes
sit side by side
watching, waiting for
the action to begin

four wheels
a red stripe and yellow lights
the bat mobile's butler

call the strippers next door
hide the drugs under
the floor boards
i think trouble got out again

there is a lonely cop
sitting in his car on the corner
eating a sandwich
drinking a pop
maybe doing paperwork
but he never looks up

and misses it all.

DISPOSABLE CAMERAS

the first time i met you
was on a pathway from
the parking lot to a
friend's apartment block

i still don't know
how you knew her

you were carrying a
full length mirror

i was already drunk
so, when i spotted you
i started running from
my friends, towards you

and when i got close
i blurted between
panted breaths
"what... what are... what the...
where are you going with a
12 pack and a mirror?!"

you laughed at me as i
slurred out *"weiirrrddooo"*

we both laughed
and later
you helped me
stand on the keg

called me short

i shot you a middle finger with
my one free hand
then asked what you were
going to do with the mirror

you said you thought you'd
leave it for the party

that was
before selfies, well

we had selfies—we just had to wait

that night
the hangover
and one hour if
we wanted to see
the aftermath of
our egos.

my roommate
wanted to leave
i said goodbye as
you wrote
down your number

we hung out a few
more times after that
until we both stopped
calling back.

HAPPY HOUR

"i am afraid," you said
then chugged the rest of
both our drinks and
motioned to the bar for
a couple more

when they arrived
you carried on
"i am already cynical
 and now
 it's just like
 i fucking hate women
 i know what they are capable of"

i nodded
took a sip and
lit a cigarette
then feeling obligated
said, *"ya*
 women are bitches"

you didn't respond

instead we sat in silence
watching drunk college girls on
the beach bicker over whose turn
it was with the selfie stick

and when
the sun set
you left
saying you
were

supposed to meet up
with this girl from
the internet

i stayed a bit longer
then left too.

TWO STEPPING

you look good
you really do

but we are grown

and now there are
just too many
other options

you look good
you really do

but this pop song
blaring through
speakers older
than us, has more
stout than you

and this beer dripping
down my hands and legs
as i dance back and forth
has a better chance of
getting me to stop all the
petty nonsense than you do
too

honestly, you should know
i'll go home with anything in
this bar but

you.

YOU CAN BE THE IDIOT

maybe
just maybe
a small percentage of
what we agreed
this whole thing would
be based on is
out of calculation
out of control
out of batteries

and if this is so
i am ok

as long as
it is you

you are the one
spinning
irrationally
into nothing

for if it is me
to have these revelations
to have these moments of instability

i want to be
no part of it.

THE USUAL

"you never take the
fucking compliment"

you said that, then stubbed
out your cigarette

the last one i might add
but right now
i wouldn't

you had promised me the
last bit of it
but i won't mention it

you got up
walked towards the kitchen

i heard the fridge door open
the rustle of cans in cardboard
then the door slam

and
cardboard
hit drywall

i think you were
aiming for the
garbage bin
but then again
i won't chime in

i know it's me
the joker

the one that
can't take
anything serious except
a big o' toke-r

oh
me
oh
my

i
messed
it
up
with
another
guy.

I GET CRABBY WHEN THE A/C BREAKS

our limbs hang
out the
window as
two box fans
blast us

it was hell getting
this lit

i take a
few hits then
pass it over

you take a hit
and in between coughs
ask
"you smoke
 before bed?"

"yes"

you cough out *"fascinating"*

it sounded patronizing
so, i snarl back
"i don't see why"

you shake your
head and
grab
some water

after chugging half the bottle

you laugh out
"that i am
interested in
your life?"

glaring at you through
my sweaty eyelashes
"i see what you did there"

looking genuinely confused
you ask, *"what you mean?"*

but i don't buy it
"you know
damn well what
i mean"

having lost your
doobie privileges at
this point

i take
a couple more drags
then carry on *"it's not*
                    fascinating"

i take another drag
"to smoke weed
before bed or altogether really"
and another drag
"you call it my 'life'
and that you are
interested in it"
and another drag
"point for you
for caring"

you just stare at me

then say
i sound angry
and snatch back
the doob

this time focusing on
smaller hits—you don't cough

fucking bravo—i am clapping for you

you ignore me
and ask
*"i am just interested
  can i be?"*

taking back the doob, *"can you what?"*
i ask between puffs, *"be interested?"*

i take a long drag
then answer for you
 "of course"

you grin like a child, making me laugh

i spit smoke into your face
and say, *"i want you to be"*

you cough
sit back in your chair
remove your
feet from
the window and say
"thank you"

i feel uneasy
and queasy

i take a few more drags
then stub it out in
an old coffee cup
and say, *"you're welcome"*

afterwards
we both sit in
silence

sweating.

IT'S OK TO NOT BE OK

"why don't you care?"
you screamed that while
trying to light a cigarette

i think, it would have killed you
if you knew, it was making you look
like a girl

i sat down and reached
for the pack but
you had it snatched
my fingers didn't even
get close

i looked you in the eyes
and cautiously admitted
"it's just something, i can't bear"

you handed me the lit cigarette from
your mouth, *"what are you on about?"*

i took a drag
embracing the lag, i held the smoke in
wishing it was a joint
wishing i didn't have to make my point
*"i just... i don't have it in me to care
anymore"*

with that confession
i could see your desperation turn to doubt
you turned away from my face and said
"we don't work anymore, do we?"

i shook my head but you couldn't
see with your back to me

taking my silence as
the answer, you picked up
your pants and left.

MONOLOGUES

are you listening?

i don't think you are, you are slurring
out something off topic, over me, though
you had asked—me. and now, you can't
even hear me, cause of your own voice.

i am bored.
taking a hit from your abandoned cigar
and inhaling it, habits, trying to
drown down the cough with my drink
i spit it up and nearly choke
at least, i got a head spin from
it—more than usual

you are still talking, you don't notice
me start texting, but when i stand up
you grab my arm, regaining my focus
saying something about opening a
bakery, that we would be happy, ha!

bullshit. i am pretty sure
you had just, like 2 minutes ago
asked what i thought of jamie oliver
and i said he was ok, but i would never
work in a kitchen again.

again, are you listening?
i don't think you do, and i
don't blame you

your voice has always been
louder than mine.

THE FRONT LAWN SHOW

you were waving your hand out the
car window, like you were a conductor
"you drive me crazy!"

and i am just not
playing fast enough
"well the way i see it"
i said
laughing
"i did you a favor
  everyone should
  go crazy"

you turned your car on
as i went on, *"it's healthy"*

the roar of your
engine let me know

you
did not
think so.

SIGNALS

they are wrong

it is all
wrong
until i figure it out.

then they are right

wrong
except, when right?

i
hate
you.

I WANT ALL THE DRINKS
stories of a greedy girl

i
am
always
saying
too much

you
are
always
saying
too little

but
when
there is
booze around

everything feels
just perfect

and right.

ANNNND, THERE GOES THE NEIGHBORHOOD

i say go away, you say no.
i say go away, you say no.
and then it starts

a few beats hit
the stereo
the airwaves
the table
the rising smoke
and then my ears

a few beats and i'm hearing all
the lessons you've been collecting
since we first started meeting

fleeting
beating

i think i should take a seat
while i meet my heart for
the first time

maybe i can be mine
maybe i can love myself

i think it's all possible when i have
the comforts of this bottle

throttle
put down the throttle
i want to feel like a model
my hair in the wind, and you

you are my binge.

bend and bend.
the seat belt in my neck and
your hand on my thigh.

lie and lie.
i am forgetting there is a
word that explains this.

i don't care if you lie,
if you can also give me

a goodbye.

PARTY GAMES

face to
the ground

laid out

thinking of
all the forgotten weed that
now neighbors these kind of
brown synthetic fibers

whole nugs lost to
the chaos in a
carpet that never
gets cleaned

you kicked
my shoe
told me
to get up

but i couldn't
i felt glued

it could have been the
bong hits

it could have been the
whiskey

it could have been my
pride melting away
after losing drunk jenga and
having *"fuck you!"*

screamed at me by
a dozen alcoholics as
i was being forced to
kiss the floor

it does feel nice though

not being attached
to you.

WHEN DO MY BENEFITS KICK IN

we started off as friends

laying on your back
pants unzipped
"are you good at handjobs?"

i rolled my eyes
"ya
  i guess, i mean
  i've never had a guy
  not cum, so i guess
  that vouches for
  something
  right?"

you grabbed the bottle of lotion
quite violently from my nightstand
"hold out your hands
  and stop talking about
  other men"

i did what you said

but with attitude
and a slight pout
"whatever
  you were the one
  that asked"

i rubbed my hands together
then slid them in
to your boxers.

IN THE WIND

ash swirls
around us
like snowflakes

i stick out
my thumb
to catch one

while you are
busy searching
your pockets
for a phone.

GIVE ME THAT TANQUERAY TONGUE

in the back garden of your
mate's place, you kept
asking about the states
telling me your mum's
uncle's friend's wife is
from a town in michigan
do i know her?

all i could taste was
your thick accent
and some sick rising
i ended up walking away

a few hours later
wasted

i was upstairs, in line for
the only bathroom in
a 3-story house

you came up behind me
smacked my ass
then fell a few feet into
the wall, by this time
you had stopped
speaking altogether

i think we could really
get on with each other

but never sober.

BEING HONEST HERE

at the bar
trying to get
another vodka with
orange and cranberry when

you shoved into me
saying sorry

apologizing and
declaring my
bud light soaked blouse—ok

but it wasn't

i wasn't.

you are no
leader

i am no
liar

things are not—ok.

THE 8TH GRADE DANCE AFTER PARTY

i tilted my head back until
it hit something

you had glow in the dark
stars covering your ceiling

the fruit punch was
just vodka

i think

i should have got a
ride home from
one of the katies'
and their mom

katie m.
katie p.
one katie
two katie
red katie
blue katie

my head is reeling
and now i will have to
walk home
and maybe this
make-out session
wasn't such a clever idea

right now i am
tasting stomach and
bits of heart in my mouth

someone told me
it was an obligation of
mine to give you
a 'blowy'
after we
have been
dating
one month

that is why i stayed

i tilted my head back
thinking, if i didn't stay

you wouldn't either.

THE CIRCLE JERK

tip and sip

*"if you're upset
it means
you're weak"*

you said that
while arguing that
you weren't arguing
with me

do you even
remember what
a point is?

BABYSITTING THE BOTTLE

little sips
against
big gulps

i never
stood a
chance.

EGOS, VERTIGO, & VIRGOS

observation
conservation
you took a vacation
to vatican city
came back
talking all witty
and apparently
'over my head'

as we laid
in *my* bed

because you
could never afford
your own place
on a traveler wage

you said
i needed to be
enlightened
i needed to get out
and see things

oh
i wish i
knew as much as you

i felt like i
had no other choice

i turned over towards you
and said
"babe

don't worry about me
i have already been to
a higher place, several times"

you grinned and
nodded for more

pleading for me to
scratch and knead
that big ass ego
of yours

but i
wouldn't

instead i said
"just not with you"
then got up

grabbed the plate
from the microwave
and the straw out of
your big gulp.

FREIGHT TURNER

with the rest
i stand in empty bars

chugging vodka.
though i have always
hated vodka
it's what i deserve
when i stand here
with the rest

in empty bars
night after night.

though i have
always hated
vodka

i have
always liked
it more than
any sober
thought of

well fuck

you know it's you.

I DON'T KNOW YOUR MIDDLE NAME

softly fading in,
fiercely storming out on me,
you're always a flame.

ALL MY EXES ARE MESSES

trying to adjust my
bra strap in the guest
bathroom and
you walk in
smiling
saying you were
looking for me

i'm pretty drunk
but can still tell
you are rolling

you push me up
against the
granite countertop
your step-mom had
just got put in

and i push back

she always treated me
like garbage, she's a total bitch
but she's not who i am
upset with—it's you

for saying you
would save me one

and clearly
you had both.

THE TRIANGLE

it is boring

for all the time
we have been
spending in bars

drinking beer
and smoking cigarettes

i think i still
spend more time
staring at the door

i am not sure what
i am looking for

but there has
to be more than this.

CHAPTER TWO
DINNER WINE

LOUD DOES NOT EQUAL RIGHT

slow it down and have
a drink; lets not say every
little thing we think.

WORD VOMIT

sweat bubbles burst
against my
humid forehead

you have been
talking all night long about
things and more things

i just can't get
interested in them
and yes
i am drunk

so i am not quite sure what
all this means

are we over?

or do bubbles burst
differently when
i am sober?

NOT MY FAULT

we were drinking
cheap sangria

the kind that comes
in a gallon jug
the glass ones
and after some
like just
a little bit
you passed out

i got bored

thought maybe i
would keep drinking until
my tongue started to
look dark red

then get up
turn the lights off
air down to 68
climb in bed

but it never did

and when the bottle was
gone and wasted
so was i

that damn tongue of mine.

YOU TALK AND I LISTEN

we go on and on
at 3 am about politics
and life, as if the
two are similar

we go on and on
with our own
opinions, quick to
trump each other's

"we just, i feel like, we
 introduced caitlyn jenner
 into society like, well like
 it was something normal," you said
and picked up a packet of chips

i know you are high and drunk
so, all this is expected

you carry on, *"and like, it is just not"*
shoving your face with salt and vinegar
"ya know?"

we go on and on
about the changes we
will make in the morning, then
curse the fuck out of the sun
when it decides to rise

we go on and on
over the educational
system in america today, but then say
i think i will homeschool.

THE BALLROOM SHUFFLE

this is how it starts
i know because
that is how it started
with us

between side glances and
well-rehearsed dances

spinning
around the words
we knew would
leave us hooked
on the idea
that we could ever last.

MY TRIP TOWARDS CASABLANCA

half a gram for
75, we were
robbed—obviously

money that none of
us could afford but
we took the bag anyways

then smoked ourselves
the rest of the way to where
we needed to be

out of beer
out of liquor

he was on your
handlebars as
i skated besides

laughing
i pushed in and
out and up and
down the hills i
had made up from
the driveways that
normally line
South Brevard Avenue

i heard you say *"she's gonna fall"*

and then him replying *"nah, she's good
on these"*

which i appreciated and

turned into the confidence
i used to lunge at the rack
on the back of your bike

looking for a break i

i was looking at your head not
the ground, i didn't see the rock

i flew for what seemed like
days through the air just thinking
"you stupid shit
 protect your face"

JUST SHUT UP

english

we both
speak english

but sometimes
i feel like my
words are coming
out in a
language
that only turns
your eyebrows in
and your lips down

i know it is
because i am
out of reach
and your hands
cannot find me

we have always
had better success
communicating

when our bodies were
involved and our words were
left to fend for themselves.

IS THIS WHAT YOU HAD IN MIND?

stale smoke surrounds us
you're on the bottom, looking
right into my eyes.

HOUSE PARTIES AT 28

albeit
i am lit

here dancing
heavily in a
living room

two floors above traffic
one floor above a palm reader
and the same as a boy i
went to school with

in the bathroom
a scene laid out on
the counter

a knock on the door
i answered and he
squeezed through
giving me the
'real' sugar

we talked
him sitting on a ledge near the tub
me on the back on the toilet

until a girl
forced us
out

needing
to pee

after smashing a beer bottle accidently
i bounced around energetically
making driving maneuvers
with my arms

thinking
he turned out alright

not a loser
at all.

GO ON, PICK THE SCAB

i met him at a party, and then again, and
again, he was everywhere
he liked to wear lacoste and thought
jeff ross was funny, high when he
said that—still, we got along
despite not liking each other.
i think it was because neither of us
put an effort in to care, or maybe it was
because the sex was animalistic and
fantastic—either way, something
kept us both coming back

i'd steal him expensive shirts from stores
we both didn't shop at, he would
buy me something other than gas station
beer to drink, i was nineteen
i would bring him with me to frat parties
and help him swindle free drugs from all
the girls and then
let him drink all my beer when we
lost the games i swore i was
"somewhat decent" at, he took me to
get my nosed pierced, then didn't get out
of my bed for a week
he would steal special brownies from his
friends for me, i'd let him have half
while he sat in my bath for hours
i sat on the counter reading him my
cosmopolitan magazines, he was a scorpio
we would go to random parties in my
apartment complex and pretend we didn't
know each other, see who

could hook up with someone else first
both end up by
the alcohol, id steal a bottle while he
covered me, we were really fucking messy

back and forth we went for years
until he moved away
until i moved away

and now
nearly a decade later, i see him
drunk across the bar
blocking one of two exit doors

i get up

making my
way over.

THE COOKIE MONSTER

you mess with my head
almost like
you know what you are doing
with it

putting your hands
in a jar
that wasn't meant
for you

telling me
we haven't
properly met yet

i know you

i said, i know boys like you

but you say, i am a fool

i should
shut my mouth and
show you
what kind of things
i like to/can do.

THE TOOTSIE ROLL POP OWL

no tricks
no picks
no alligator dicks

we both agreed
not to chase each other

we both agreed
not to want each other

but we do.

so tell me

how many licks
will it take
until we realize this?

AFTER THE BAR BUT BEFORE WE SLEEP

we are as
civil
as the
situation
is

and
it
never
is

"just shut up
  and take your pants off"

you said that while
taking off yours

i am always
talking too much
by this point

so i said nothing
and just did
what you asked.

OUTSIDE IN THE COLD

embarrassingly
the end of our
doobie got caught on
my lip and tugged a
bit when i tried to
part the two and i
know you liked it

i don't know if it
was the struggling i
went through, or that
my lip had wavered
on where it wanted to
go, for once

either way, i know
you liked it

i know this because
you made it perfectly clear.

TREATS

pile on to me like
scoops of ice cream—i'm greedy

give me all you have.

THOUGHT BUBBLES FROM A FIGHT

i know you
like it best
when i
don't talk;
sometimes
my words hurt
your feelings

i know that you
like this best
because you
have told me;
sometimes
my words can
break you down

but i like
it best
when we
talk;
sometimes
you forget
to talk

and i like this
best because it's
when we
get along;
sometimes
we forget its best
when we get along

A NIGHT IN WITH BUD & BOOZE

smoke floats
drifting into
somersaults that
bounce off the
lampshades and
pictures hanging
from your wall

it's slow
it's so slow
slow
sloooooooow

i think i
feel the
trampoline in
my chest

they are
playing there too

flips
i think

backflips into the trees

i feel
a bit
sickly.

BEST WESTERN

leave your comments in
my ear; i am here waiting
wanting to please you.

COMPROMISE

late
like 4 am
so early rather

you called me baby and
said you could date me
and we would fall in love
then fight
breaking up within
a year

i laughed and
said probably, ya

you took a deep breath through
the telephone before
blowing out an
exhausted, *"fuck"*
followed by
"maybe... we could
  make this work"

i surpassed another laugh
and settled with
"only if you know how to
  delete maybes."

HOT COALS

heel
    toe

heel
    toe

        alternate
            rotate
          liberate
        and skate
        on by, but

        never
        never
        never

        hesitate.

UNDERSTANDINGS

"that's my beer"
i said with daggers
in my eyes

"oh"
placing it back down
this time slightly more in front of me
"it's ok" you picked the other can up
took a swig, then smiled
"i don't mind a bit of your saliva"

i grabbed mine, took a swig
"well"
taking another
"i do"

you burrowed your eyebrows
took a gulp of your beer
then said, a bit unsteadily
"you don't want my saliva?"

i shook my head while taking a sip
then said, *"i mind you*
 drinking all my beer"

you laughed
raised your can up a bit
and said, *"fair enough"*

THE DANCE FLOOR

this beat
is ruining
this moment

both your hands
are in places
my clothes
are refusing
to cover

i am moving
swaying even
to where you
are going

though i think i
would rather
be anywhere else

but i am drunk

and the choices
are limited
to where my
head will fall

this beat
is ruining
this moment.

CHANGE OF SUBJECT

*"have some water
you're drunk"*

i rolled my eyes at you
grabbed the plastic cup
you were holding out to me
sat down
took a sip
then lit a ciggy

you asked if i had eaten
i replied that i had been
out at the bars since 3, and
to not be silly—course i didn't

you perked up and started
snapping towards my purse
*"you sneaky girl
not telling me"*

*"it's in my bra
hold on"*
i took a few more drags
then stubbed the ciggy out on
a brick wall behind me

i got up and slid the
baggy into my cigarette pack
then tippy-toe-kissed your
cheek while slipping my hand
into your back pocket

you smiled

then left
for my car

i picked up
my purse
made my way
back to the bar
for another drink.

ha!
crisis adverted.

MAYBE I SHOULD HAVE SOME WATER

take us in stride—

i am starting to feel the
flush in my cheeks

and though you are
making me blush
with that quick
tongue of yours

these rosy tattle tails
are calling me for
what i am

drunk.

LITTLE GREEN SECRETS

"by the way
i'm out, you know i
hate letting you down
but everyone's broke
ya know"

you grabbed my thigh
and squeezed

i nodded to ease
your worries and
said it was
no problem

and really
it wasn't

i had picked up from
your buddy an hour before
(40 bucks for better stuff)

but i won't mention that.

CONFUSED

i was in between.
where the colors start to blend
and nothing is clear.

THE SNAKEBITE

some cider
some lager
a little this
a little that
really, it's better
not to ask

handing me the
pint glass, you
told me to just
drink it

i did, it
tasted like
shit and

you laughed knowing
it would, so
i spit some out on
your shoes

two fingers shot
up in the air as
you called me a cunt

i laughed and said
you were a dick

you smiled

… ya
that sums us up

I GUESS IT'S CALLED FLIRTING

speaking in
snippets and
sarcastic
quotation
marks

we
sought out
the words
each other
liked

and
let the rest
evade us

any real
conversation
is just a
distraction

right?

TOO MUCH MOSCATO

bed sheets have been dismantled
the lamp is scattered on the floor next
to our emptied wine bottle, the lightbulb
is still flickering—i can see it in
the black of your eyes

my socks are still on

"it tastes like
  candy and goes
  down like water"
they warned

but i have never been
satisfied sleeping in
a stranger's bed when

my mind is racing and
i am working on

my come
      d
        o
         w
           n.

I LIKE THE WAY YOU TALK

you poked me in
the ass with
your pool stick to
get my attention

told me to listen

how'd ya know?
i put my hand on
the glass
squinting while
steadying my stance

how'd ya know?
this is the song i
needed to hear.

THE AUDITION

kicking my shoes
towards a crowded area

i took over the space

it was probably the drugs
but at the time

i thought i
was something special
was something different

twirling and swirling
hands pushing my
hips side to side

i never took my eyes
off you.

FIESTA HAVANA

wine splashed out of
your glass and into my mouth

i nearly lost it
but you were wasted
i could taste it

i grabbed the glass
from you and
drank it before

you had time to react

i was hoping it
would sober you up a bit

but it didn't

you smiled
swayed
then grabbed
my tit

it made me laugh

i like when you do that
and you know it.

YOU SAID THIS

*"for some reason
i can't finish
in the shower"*

for some reason
that turned me on

for some reason
i took that as a
personal challenge

for some reason
my clothes needed off

for some reason
the water broke free

for some reason
when i grabbed your hand
and led you to the bathroom

you didn't hesitate
to finish.

NIGHTS AT THE BEACH

swirling grains
of sand
and
mouthfuls of
salty hair

we wade into the
water and you
take my hand

knowing

i get scared.

THE MESSES

sat over my smith-corona
with ink on my fingertips
trying delicately to pull
out the ribbon i had just
punched holes in

finishing
and closing the lid
i say how much i
love a fresh ribbon
how i feel like i
can write and write
anything i fucking please
and the smell
i really like
the smell
and i seem to
always forget how
bold the words
are supposed to be

you looked up from your book
and smirked, then looked at my hands
"do your fingers have ink on em?

i looked down at them, then back at you
"yes"

you marked your place in the book
put it on the bedside table and got up
"that's messy, come here"

so, i did.

THE RIGHT KIND OF DRUNK

sheets sway from our bed
fabric dancing in the wind

we   are   the   clothespins.

REASSURING THE "YA, SURE"

i will say
something you like
and then
you will say
"really?"

i will
roll my eyes
and say
*"ya
  really"*

you will say
"thanks"

and then we will
go back to before

go back
to you
thinking you are
not good enough

go back
to me
thinking up ways
to prove it

that we both are.

70% MADE OF BULLSHIT

i think my problem might
be the whole honesty stuff.
i thought maybe
it was pride, but
if we are now being honest
i am not honest with myself

there is no pride
there was never pride
i made it all up in my head
but don't blame me just yet
everyone else was doing it too

i mean, everyone in my head
was doing it too

look, i don't think
i am drunk enough

usually, i need to be
drunker than this

stumbling towards my drink
i put down the darts
take a chug and miss a bit

it falls to my shirt and
into my bra

you take your turn
triple 17 and a 15
the last one hit the wall

i step up and throw it before
looking, bull's-eye (in the green)

maybe, i am drunk enough
after all.

NOT UNTIL SIMON SAYS

with my restless feet,
i am static, here waiting,
for you to say go.

THAT LOCAL BAR ON CHRISTMAS EVE

i am a bit
insecure but
when i
am in the
bathroom
throwing up and
i know you are
outside
at the bar
getting a drink and
girls are talking
you up, that

i am ok

i know this because i
have the bag you need

to get you through a
night like this.

DEAL OR NO DEAL

i need to
unwind, and you
know how to
make me

"take off
 your shirt," you say
"let me give you a massage"

i know nothing comes for free
but right now, my back is killing me

i take off my shirt, lay face down
placing the pillow under my head

"take it all off"
you actually whined that

i tried to bargain that i just
wanted my back done
but you were having none of that
ripping off my jeans
giving me a grin

i forgot what i was
trying to argue as
your
hands
slid along my skin

that is
until the end

when i got interrupted by you
whispering in my ear

"my turn."

THEY TREAT YOU LIKE FAMILY

i am practically laying on top of
the counter by now, the cashier isn't
even blinking, and i am realizing that
recently, i have been doing way more
squinting than reading, does that
say $63 or $53?

after a while i give up trying to
see the labels, pick the prettiest
bottle and pay

leaving the liquor store with the
tequila for my brother's birthday, i
spot a couple—hands ripping each
others hair out in the cab of a
ford ranger pick-up

making out or making up for something
either way, it made me want this to
be a gas station, and alcohol a
pile of scratch-offs:

sit here and

drink until i end up with something else

drink until i feel happy

this is all a lottery, right?

WHAT THIS IS

it's a duel

prearranged
by our
prehistoric
habits

the ones
that cause
us to
passive
aggressively

want
each
other's
pants off.

CHAPTER THREE

TOP SHELF WHISKEY

SHOTS!

we should curtsy past
the reasons why we won't last
let's love hard and fast.

DAY DRUNK WITH MARGARITA ON MY SHIRT

sorta like a splash pool
i will dip my toes in
but i am keeping my hair dry

we can try
we can take this as it comes
but i am not about to
get soaking wet

…all this in my head
   of course

the reality…
i am partaking in a
prolific texting situation
about a chair and
you pulling my hair
when i get one saying
*"you've made me wanna
   masturbate
   on my lunch break"*

with that i realized
any composure i am
pretending to possess
has been lost to your penis

and i am
drenched.

STRAWBEERY PAPERS

i have had
too much to drink
i have had
too much to think

and you

something i never get
enough of

it what
i always want

even when

i am full off
something else.

USE ME

mechanically—
you are the plastic pencil
i'm pieces of lead.

RECALLING ALL IKEA LIFE RAFTS

your morning eyes
never lie
and the evening ones
always do

i find bliss in
the silence
of a manual typewriter
but also comfort in
the hum of electric ones

if you are asking
about me
forgiving you

don't be daft
i always do

don't be daft
i always come back
to you.

YOU'RE SITTING ACROSS THE BAR
& I CAN'T STOP STARING

it's just that i

i would rather be
the one to cause
chaos in you

than be part of the crowd
that left you alone.

TRUTH SERUM

i am
flushed
blushed
please rush
me to bed

i've had too
much to drink
and it's all
gone to
everything
i've said and

too much of
you has gone
to my head.

HOW I CARE ABOUT YOU

please pass
over another
modelo
please hand
me that tray
dear lover
i wanna
roll one up
and forget today
our brains
have had
enough

let's
lay here
and just
have a
little think
or a good
long blink

sink
yourself
into that chair
and take a hit
here take this
then let it go

i hate seeing
you so stressed

did you know?

THE VIPER BROTHERS GOT ME MARTINI DRUNK

"well
don't ya look
fucking fancy"

your brother said
that aggressively

startling me, and
forcing me to drop the
ciggy i was trying to sneak
then watched as i scrambled around
like an idiot, trying to pick it up

you were chuckling, the way i
think maybe a bear would—like pooh
you remind me of him, always sticking
your hands in my honey hole

ya know what though

that slutty honey
likes it, likes the

feel of needy hands.

THE FONT BAR

under neon lights
on top of worn in concrete
next to angry gusts of bus exhausts

you kissed
my chapped and alcohol infused lips

we laughed

it's always this way
when we say

"only one drink."

PAUL

raided
faded

you
have
me
sedated

and
far
too
gone
for

my
control
to
be
reinstated.

HAND TRICKS

the whole time
my attention
had been on
your mouth
those lips
the way your tongue
slips slightly
between your teeth
when you pronounce
any word ending with 'th'

but i should have
kept my eyes on
your liberated hands
slyly sliding their way

closer
and
closer
to me

(up my leg and
 under my skirt)

with
each
breath
we
inhaled.

LINED UP FOR MORE

with tangled hair and
flimsy limbs, i make my way
to you for seconds.

3:49 AM – POST BAR

in a 24-hour tescos
in the readymade aisle
looking at the ingredients
on sandwiches because
england really likes
mayonnaise, and i really don't

you grabbed my hand
i grabbed a plain cheese bap
then asked
"how late can
  you get beer here?

you laughed
dropped my hand
and checked your phone
"not this late
  sorry love"

i pouted

you kissed my lips
then grinned
"you taste like
  candy floss"

i smiled and
licked my lips
"ya
  i think it was
  that last shot"

you took my
hand and
led us towards
the pharmacy

my stomach was
growling and
my eyes were
starting to waver
*"what we come
  here for anyways?"*
i moaned, annoyed

you squeezed my hand
i think more as to wake me up
than an act of endearment, then said
"condoms, sweetie"—water on my face!

i nearly forgot about
the plans i had for us

i picked up my pace and
yours

made sure to eat my sandwich
on the walk home.

THE TAILS UP PENNY

i am not supposed
to pick you
to think you are good
to question
to ask why

only accept
it is a no
it is a he's no good

but i say stop
i don't believe
superstitions
i can't

i need
to save you
to put use to you
to show you

you are significant
even when
you think
otherwise.

CPR

peculiar
pickup lines
resonated
off your tongue
and into the
vacant space
behind
my eyes.

THE CATCH UP

tiny
carbonated
bubbles
sit on
your lips

and i cannot
take my eyes
off them

talking about
your job
your family
your trips

how you think
we have changed—i don't care

i want a taste.

FOR A BOY I KNOW

sprawled out on my bed

you read aloud the
haiku i had just
written about
paper bouquets and
me and maybe you
before tossing it
on the floor
"fuck writing
  shit for people"

i sat up and
looked at
the floor then
towards you
"i like writing
  about people"

you rolled your eyes
"i meant for people
  not about people"

i laid my head back
down on the pillow
"i don't do that but
  ya know, if it's about them
  it's generally for them"

you got off the bed and
walked over to the
bourbon sitting
alone on the windowsill

i couldn't see you
only heard the bottle
clink against the wall
and your voice

you were sounding out
the words
fuck and *them*

i felt the need
despite knowing it
wasn't the best idea
to make it known to you
that i usually have, and
it's where i get my ideas
then laughed

you went silent
which i knew you would
then called me bukowski
with a twat
which i hadn't expected, but

i liked that
a lot

you saw and
called me out
*"it wasn't a compliment
i wasn't talking about
his writing"*

i knew what that meant
so i threw a pillow
and a *"fuck you!"*
in retaliation

you let both miss you and
then took several chugs of
your bottle before
breaking into laugher
saying you already have.

MANCHESTER

he took my hand
led me noisily through
the streets
as we walked home
to his

it was a
dying art

the way he made my heart
want to trade places with
my tongue and teeth.

THE FIRST TASTE OF GLACIER WATER

black
sometimes white
sometimes clear

you told me to
put my ciggy there
while we made out and
pretended to play pool

was there even
a stick?

you wiped me clean with
the words you had
rolling off your tongue
and i said

every word i have ever known
has gripped to the mouth of
every person i have ever known

this, feels refreshing.

AN ALL-NIGHT BINGE

dazed
hazed
ya, i blazed

stumbled through an
alleyway and on
to a road

12 grenades in my hand
one broke
covered the ground in yolk

you said
throw it

i bit my lip
and did it

the car screeched to a stop
on a four-lane highway
the light was barely
above the trees
i think it was only
6 in the morning

you ran
they ran
i froze

until you
came back to grab
my hand, we ran.

THEN BUT NOT NOW

my tank top strap
fell off my shoulder
and down my arm

you
grabbed it
corrected it
gave me a bit of hope
then left out the door

it was exactly
what i needed.

LITTLE ACCOMPLISHMENTS

everything inside
smelled of puke, so
i walked outside

and found you
sitting on a tire by
the dumpster, i pulled
a ciggy from my pocket and walked over
raising my hand up
"high five"

you slurred out
"what for?"

i lit my ciggy and told you that
for once, we aren't the drunkest.

LIQUID COURAGE

i am
swimming
through
these
bed sheets
like

i was born with
gills in place of lungs

it's freeing

before this
before you

i always had
the feeling that

i was drowning.

THE GLUTTON

please come back to bed
my arms were not done with you
and neither was i.

IT'S LIKE
IF EDWARD SCISSORHANDS DID CARTWHEELS

ears ringing with
the drum and hum of
an overwhelmed heart

i feel like the wrong things
are being silent

it's the screech
leeching onto my nerves

i see you swerve
so i lunge
as you crash

tripping and falling towards you
burning my arm
on cigarette ash

everyone looks on with faces of doom
while i fail at saving you

we are a mess
we have always been a mess
we will always be a mess

and though we are
smarter than this, we know

at least it's us, together.

HAND IN HAND

when you
look at me across

drinks
and
drinks
and
girls
and
drinks
and
smoke with

all your
gaze, with

all you got

you have never
looked more
attractive and

i have never been
more attracted
to myself.

A FAIR REVIEW

you got me hooked
on lines and whiskey
you got me scrambling
to hide the flask
from a nosy carnie

nuts and bolts
started to turn and
we started to turn

the lights were blinding
the screams were hilarious

but my stomach
wished i wouldn't
always try to
keep up with you

i wanted to puke, but
we kept spinning
so, i didn't

i lost track of where you were
i lost track of where i was

you are so good at that
you know i am—bat shit crazy

and sometimes need to escape from it.

OUR LITTLE MEETINGS

"i am thinking
about going with
that theme for
my next book"

i read it over a
half dozen times
all 5 words of it
then handed it back
grabbing your beer
"i like it"

you read it again
critiquing it again
"ya
  i think people
  like the short stuff"

handing back the beer
"i like your
  long stuff better"

you nodded
i continued
"but i like
  the stuff about me
  the most"

you laughed
"course you do"

and with that—i felt like we were both
satisfied.

A BOY NAMED JOHN

"i'd get it
 and tell nobody
 about it"

you said that
then leaned back
in a plastic
patio chair

i sat
and stared, thinking

i like him

and i know
you were talking about
manatee meat

but still

i loved that
loyalty.

PRUDE REHAB

find a way to
take it all

steal if
you need to.

LIKE A BIRTHDAY

captain & coke
all night with
your bullshit

but i kind of
liked it.

when everyone left
i asked you to stay

then we went to
my bedroom
and afterwards
had a doob
on the bit of roof
outside my window

you asked if
we could take a bath

i said no
but you could

and you did
while i sat on my sink
feeding you every other cheetos

in the morning, you left
not to be seen
for another year.

WE WALKED HERE

a lost boy in a supermarket

you are looking into the windows of
every black car you see, and i am
standing 50 feet away on the
sidewalk, staggering

laughing

i yell out
"babe!"
you turn, and
i wave

a mix of anguish and assurance
cross over your face as
you race towards me

tripping a few times on
some nasty cracks
you never look back

i say nothing
on the way home

i think you might be
embarrassed.

MY TONGUE TASTES LIKE LEMON DROP SHOTS

i am a child

i am bratty

every word that
leaves your mouth

makes me horribly
and selfishly, jealous

if it is not
my name.

IT'S A START

one of the first things
you ever said to me
"i hope you enjoy sarcasm"

it caught me off guard
being as it was a little
more direct than
i was used to
from the other boys
then again
you did not seem like
those other boys

or maybe you are

i laughed
a nervous laugh
"i do, too much"

we both grinned.

SWEETWATER

texting me from a train
asking what color my panties are

and if i would ever
move back to europe

you never cared for florida
but love spain

we are older
and different

though all this
it feels the same

i text back
"black"

its morning there
and here, i am drunk again.

FOLLOWING THE LEADER

you've got this way
of losing yourself
to a room

how it
speaks
thinks
moves
plays

what it does
you do, and i

i have this way of
losing myself to you.

IN THE CLUB

glow sticks join hands to
form a halo around
your head

maybe it's an interest in why
you are
the way you are

that keeps me here

maybe i am just lost and
any light
even yours

is what keeps me here

either way
i am stuck
i am attracted.

LITERATURE

"lit-tra-chur"

when you
look me in
the eyes
and
pronounce my
favorite words
with that accent

how do you
not expect me
to fall in love
with you

with the way
your tongue moves

perhaps you were
not ready
for this

which is
understandable

neither was i.

THE BRITS ALWAYS GET ME

it is your cheek
that keeps me
on my knees
subdued by
intrigue

it is your cheek
that comes out
after a few drinks
to say all the things
your sober mind
cancels out in a blink

it is your cheek
that has me
comfortably sitting
on the sidelines—waiting.

SMOKING THE ENTIRE CARTON
KIND OF PUNISHMENT

sat here, salivating from
the disdain that pours out
your mouth when you say
his name with mine

it sounds so tasty, and i
don't think i can resist it

knowing damn well it's no good
for my health, for my safety, i
still want it, i want you

so here is my plan
i'm gonna give you what you want
i'm gonna have it
i'm gonna have you

so much unil i'm sick
so much until i don't want a taste
so much until i don't want you.

GOING MAD

you will not settle
and neither will i—it's fine

get carried away.

ATTENTION

i think about you
late at night when
everyone starts to
leave and go home
with whoever they
have been chatting up

when me and the
girls are in the
bathroom forcing
down some more stuff

before leaving to
someone's house

its human nature, right?

it's the way things
work out

the whole concept of
not always getting
what you want

adds character, right?

all i am implying is—i crave yours.

SECONDHAND GRIEF

i don't mind
being weak
if it means
you will be
strong right now

little freckles
trickle down
your nose

trails of
smoke blow
out your
mouth

and you say
*"i'm ok
  it's ok
  life is what it is"*

and i say
nothing.

BASIC BULLSHIT MATH

you make me
weak in
the knees

but that's fine

since you
like me on
my knees.

GETTING GOT OR GETTING BY

humor me with
a puckered up
peck on the
back of my neck

wait a sec
let me
beg for more

keep the lights on
keep me turned on

i don't know *"stop"*
only *"start"*
and when to part my knees;

i can be smart

but that never
got me as far
as i like.

TURNING 29 IN A MONTH

i took a
bump then
threw it up in
a bin

along with
my pizza
lunchable.

i am so glad
we are getting lit

i am so glad
life goes on without

me
in
it.

THAT CERTAIN NEIGHBORHOOD

blitzed mercilessly
by your drive-by eyes, i was
dead before you left.

CHAPTER FOUR
TAP WATER
(the hangover)

A GHOST THOUGHT

i am silently sleeping

while you are creeping

like a blanket of fog

towards where i have
my head laid

towards where i have
my bed made.

SOBER TAKEBACKS

tit for tat
pit for pat

the next day we
took our turns
proclaiming

"i didn't say that!"

A TINY LIGHTSWITCH

my fish was
belly up in
his tank when
i got home from
work today

his name was bob
and i never got
a damn goodbye

he was happy
i think
i hope

until he
wasn't anymore

change always
comes too quickly
for me.

THE HANGOVER BLUES

a lost shoe, a
who's who situation, a
borrowed phone to call mine, a
found purse, i left.

the squinting, the
headache and dry mouth, the
unidentified blood on my shirt, the
guilt i had towards my
one bare foot, i pouted.

a shower, a
doobie and bottles of water, a
thermostat on 68, a
tightly wrapped
blanket burrito, i hate myself.

WHY DO I GO OUT?

wines, lines, bad timing
i should've stayed home with papers
notebook and rolling.

ALICE

an
endless
stream of
dirty syllables

spill out the
mouths of
an endless cycle of
dirty
boys that
endlessly leave
me feeling

dirty.

PLAYING NICE

tangled hair and a
somewhat drowsy stare

my feet have only now
touched the ground

you stand there hovering
close to your car keys

my head is clogged with
last night's binge and
every time i blink
my whole body cringes

i know what you are
waiting to say

i have said it many times
i have heard it a lot too

but in all this daylight
in my sober haze of self-hate
i really wish you would
pardon my behavior
and just go

oh
and please
make it a tiptoe.

DRINKS WITH AN EX

sat across the table from you

i felt like a child trying to
act natural while holding their
parents wine glass

i took a sip while you
took what i had left

sip by sip
bit by bit

and when we
stumbled to bed

everything was empty.

DRUNK SEX WITH AN EX

in the grass
hair fanned out

i trace clouds with my finger
pretending they are something else

in my bed
hair twirled and curled

i trace your lips with my finger
pretending they said something else.

FUNGI

you always did the talking, it is what
you are good at
i like to listen

"let's split and eighth
 you can be a lightweight"

i did as i was told

the first cap tasted similar to
what i imagine
mud covered styrofoam would be like

my face must have
expressed what my dehydrated tongue
could not

"if you don't like it
 put em between the Doritos
 it'll help ya not gag"

i did as i was told

i choked them down
then looked you in the eyes
and you winked
like you always do

"come on
we should go outside
you need air
we could all use some

oh, and remember not to
look in the mirror when you go pee"

i did as i was told

following everyone to the backyard
i could feel it already
then you mentioned something about
the plants having personalities

i was gone
(flying)

s
  c
    a
     l
      l
       i
        n
         g walls

where is
greg?

clouds
 f
  a
 l
  l
from
the sky

eating potato chips

177

in a
green robe

play
  keep
    away
from
mirrors and

drive docks like speedboats until we reach the l y
                                              p a
                                                ground

the things i have done
just for peeks and
weak glances into
where that
mind of yours
comes from—astounds me.

ABOVE AVERAGE

this place was built in 1985
but as i lay here
stoned
on this disgusting floral carpet
looking up at
a lamp that screams 1973
i am starting to doubt
everything you ever told me

why try to impress me
if you are only
going to lie
to me?

BEDROOM MISTAKES

"are you satisfied?"
you asked that as
you were sitting up to
grab the
ciggy pack from
your pants

i waited until
you sat down on
the windowsill to
answer *"no"*
then laughed

you did not like that—flicking the
barely smoked ciggy out
you crossed the room in a
flash and smacked my ass

i let a yelp out, laughed
then grinned. so you
slapped it again
saying *"what you mean...no!"*

i wiggled out of
your grasp and
sprung to my feet

grabbed your shirt and
slid it over my body for
a bit of protection and
maybe a bit of courage

"that one was all
  you buddy"
i pointed to your waist

you weren't laughing

i searched the floor for
my panties and when i
looked back at you…

i don't think you
thought i was funny

made me think of
something my ma
used to tell me
"if a boy doesn't give you
  a good time but asks
  just lie, they are
  sensitive too"

i kept looking at you, though
you were now looking out
the window

i may be mediocre with putting
words onto paper, but when it
comes to my mouth—i'm the worst.

THERE IS NO DENYING A CONFESSION

a bit of beer
dripped off
my lip as
you were saying
*"i thought you
   gave that stuff up"*
and pointed towards the
plate on my kitchen counter

i caught it
in a lick
and carried
on dodging your
inquiries regarding
my Friday night
"i have—most of the time"

you grabbed your
drink and called me a nutcase

i made a sour puss face
and said whatever

you tried reassuring me
saying it sounded fun though

i am sure you were
sincere but i
of course, took it
as patronizing and
took my
hands off the table

"ya ya"
i said and looked around

you kept digging
*"you must be mad on it
  be interesting to see"*

i took a minute before
giving myself back over to
your burrowing brown eyes

and this interrogation
*"ya, i can get crazy
  talk a lot"*

hahahahaha
you laughed
"can get?"

since i wasn't getting it
you clarified
*"you're already
  crazy on booze"*

i took a sip of
my drink and
thought it over

then agreed, *"that's true."*

THE HANGOVER LAMES

i am dead
recovering in unconscious
and when i am alive
though brief
i am blue

covered in
the bruises my
nose got me

testing
testing
i need more
resting

i am
regretting 4 am
i am
regretting him

and i just don't understand why
i won't behave.

YOU LIKE WHEN I DANCE FOR YOU

we were
in the parking lot
of a texico

and maybe
it was too soon
for a conclusion
i just didn't want
you to forget

you don't have to
go that way
if you don't want to
is all i heard
escape your lips

watch my hip
take a dip

i really want
to be fair

so here is
your truth

i have never cared
i am always scared.

THANK YOU FOR THE 42 CENTS

time doesn't
always heal

sometimes it just
takes your youth

sometimes it just
takes your mind

sometimes it just
takes your smile

and all you
are left with

fading words
fading faith

that you will ever
make it out

of the places
time got you into.

THE KOOL-AID

this reminds me

i taste you in
every cigarette i
drunkenly devour

and boy, do i
quickly sour
when i realize
it ain't you

just tobacco and
the forever changing
number of
chemicals
placed in
these sticks, but

whatever it is
i will take it

if it
tastes like you.

IT'S LIFE

the things you want
do not always want you too
and the things that want you
you do not always want back

but the things you need
have a way of finding you

and sometimes all you need
is a good slap in the face
to make you stop wanting
all the things that

are not meant for you
in the first place.

THE TIME IT WAS WHAT IT WAS

everyone is talking
about the situation
and i can't help
thinking it's me with
the most to learn

bent over
to get my coat

you slapped
my ass

i called you
a dick

you said you
liked that

i said i
did too

and then i
went home with you.

YELL AT ME, I LIKE IT

show
teeth

show
tongue

show
me the
backside of
your lips

show
off your
3 cavities

show
where you
used to have
tonsils

show
how everything
meets the back of
your nostrils

show
me anything except
a closed mouth.

THE PARKING SPOT OUT FRONT

i run my mouth
too much and say
things i shouldn't

then sometimes i
don't say anything
at all

not sure
which is worse.

IN THE NAME OF ART

coil around my
wrist and press
down until the
ink pops out

that is why i
bother talking
to you

my muse
my little heart
breaker you.

BAD WORDS

i know at some point
tonight you will succumb
to sleep and i will be left
here with only my thoughts

and that's OK

possibly then i can
get something on paper
other than the utter
bullshit i spew to

please you.

HABITS

i have tendencies
to outwit all the good things
it's a bad habit.

ADVICE FROM THE SUSPECT

you said that someone
can only win

shot for shot

no one cares about
the cue
no one cares about
the 8 ball

you said that it's

shot for shot

and i should
learn that now.

THE REALIST

it is
the alteration
between the
two that has
me hypnotized

stuck here in
static between
the synchronized
inhales of your breath

no escapes
no breaks

maybe i will
see you tomorrow

but
probably
not.

WORDS

fuck
i love words
when they aren't from
your mouth

syllables and
consonants playing
tic tac toe with my
maybe, well i dunno

you know

maybe i am not
who i think

maybe i am just
as horrible

as you.

WHEN FINE MEANS FINE

you
have
never
had
the
guts
and
that
is
OK
since
i
have
only
ever
cared
about
myself.

A MIDNIGHT SNACK

fishing around the
doob ends left in
an ashtray

trying to find a
solution for insomnia

in bed, you stir
in this chair, i slump down

fearing you will wake
and find me still sitting

with all your
unanswered questions.

OUR LAST WORDS

i asked calmly, though i admit
it was a bit abrupt
"why are you so mean?"

you replied in the opposite direction
arms flapping, as if you were drowning
"what the hell did i say!"

i mentioned something
about your tone

you told me, while shutting the door
we are done

but staying in my fashion, i whispered
just loud enough, *"have fun."*

FOR TONIGHT

i have just choked up a
bit in the bathroom before
writing this

but that's ok, right?
but that's what you want, right?

me to be held up on
any syllable that
sounds similar
to you

i will slip out
"oh!
  that reminds me
  so much of him…"

you will say
"shut your face"

and i will

because you are here
and my bed is made.

BUT I CAN NEVER REMEMBER

when someone is
drunk

maybe coke
maybe pills
maybe worse

it really doesn't
matter

it's always something.

only when i sober up
and stop shaking in whatever
mirage the drugs and my mind has
made up

i let someone become themselves—and i

then realize
the things i think make
me, myself

don't even exist.

DURING A DRUNK FIGHT

sometimes
throw up is
easier to get out
than words

right now
is one of those
sometimes.

ON REPEAT

hit next

take a sip

inhale the beat

quiet the monsters.

THE UNDERTONE OF THE UNDERTOW

"i was happier, then"

you got up and
began collecting
the empty
beer bottles
from around
our living room

it was all in a
lazy, unrushed
motion and

it was as if
you hadn't just
confessed that

then
is not
now.

THE NIGHT YOU SLEPT ON THE COUCH

find me between
the sheets
voice hoarse
with morning

put your hands
in my knotted hair—and pull

drench my tongue
with desire

make me find
the words

you need to hear.

BURNT

finger by finger
i loosen my grasp, and take
back my damaged hand.

STEPPING ON THE CRACKS

i walked home

eight blocks
because i didn't want to
stay with you

and on the walk home
i listened to the
waves crash against
the sand dunes

it remined me
of you
of us

something so natural
something so destructive

one
never
without
the
other.

THROWING UP ON THE DANCE FLOOR

i want you
staring at me

but right now
i wish you wouldn't

i am
a car wreck

usually i would
appreciate your
rubberneck

but right now
i don't

privacy
would be much
preferred while i
am exploding to bits

just keep moving

you
can't
save
this.

THE HOT GUY AT THE BAR

forget all about
what your parents said
regarding strangers

the talking to them
doesn't matter

it's the falling in love
with one

that will get
you hurt.

THE REUNION

10
tables
over

10
years have
moved on
without us

our eyes
locked and
struggling for

the words
we aren't allowed
to say, anymore.

WAS I ALWAYS THIS WAY?

running into you
like always

at the same bars
at the same parties
at the same weddings
at the same funerals

i see you and
i know you see me

living and
dying in
synchroneity

yet
we
never

bother with
each other.

WHEN YOU MIX ALCOHOL

drag. drag. drag.
look up and see the smoke
look up and see the same exact
view that was there before
look up and remember why
you were looking down

around. around. around.
those little curlicues make
fools of us all as
they dance with the
freedom that we fight for

dance. dance. dance.
i can't. i can't move from
this barstool if i
want to avoid puking

around. around. around.
my stomach moves when
my head does, and its
cause i know, i know i am losing.

TELLING MYSELF IT'S OK TO FUCK UP

it's hard
ya know

calculating the
words that need
to be said

it's hard
ya know

realizing that
certain words are
better for some people
than others

it's hard
ya know

deciphering the
spaces in between
the lines

it's hard
ya know

learning and living
with the times i can't

it
is
hard

ya know?

PERCEPTION

it is good to see you here
on the side of my mind, we figured
would always be desolate and forgotten

we do not see people here much
but when we do, i sure do appreciate it

though, now

we stand here
as you light the butt end of
your cigarette, for the second time

i am shouting, *"this is the life!"*

you scream, *"it is not!"*

and i don't know who
to believe.

JUST BARTENDER IT

relationships have
changed

that is what i am saying to
you as we down a few beers
and look towards the girls
leaving the beach.

i know you are hurting, and
i know i am hurting too

maybe i should say to you

something encouraging
something about how girls
aren't raging bitches

but during this sip
what i want to say is

run
fucking
run

have some fun because
girls respond best when

you don't care, so there

there is the
advice
you wanted.

NOT TONIGHT

imagine all the places
we could see
and all the people
we could be

if "can't" was not
in constant need

that dirty old slag
always nagging me.

YOU ARE A SKY DIVE
& I AM AFRAID OF HEIGHTS

try
my dad would say
over and over and
i would say i can't

try harder
he would say
and when i did
i would usually get it

you say
i don't understand you
you ask
why don't i get you

and i know it is
because i don't try.

A HEAD OF CLOUDS

a handcrafted
doob by me
a handcrafted
mess by you

one in my hand
one in my head

light up
smoke down

let this haze
cover the floor
cover the ground
you built for us

let it cover
every single thing
you have touched (here)

i want to feel weightless.

BUT WHY

why should i change
for you?

i know you are
attracted to a certain
type of girl and
i know i am
not that type

and that's ok

i don't need
you to want me

to want you back

i've never been
that type either.

TAKE ONE FOR THE TEAM

i admit

that what is
said while i am drunk

is not funny

but!

i would love
for you to recognize
my attempt

please
just don't be
a bitch

and let me
just this once

be right

even when
i am not.

UNSUPERVISED

2:37 am
booze fresh on
my breath
bruises forming on
both legs from
an unfortunate
mix-up with the
bushes outside
my apartment

i sway into the counter
trying to open
strawberry jam

pb&j sounds incredible

but my feeble
arms are
failing me

i miss you and
want you back is
all i can think

as i drift to sleep—hungry.

REJECT MIND ERASER

i don't understand
"we used to know each other"
... i'll always know you.

SNITCHES GET STITCHES

you stopped by for
a quick drink
just one

i know you had
somewhere else to be

both our feet on
the coffee table
you had a beer in
one hand and the
pages i had been
working on
in the other
"but that's just
our conversation?"
you said, confused

i tried to hide
my smile but failed
"exactly, you give
me good stuff"

you put them down and
looked towards where i
have all my notebooks lined up
"how many are related to me?"

i bit down on my lip
then admitted
"tons"

you snapped your

head back
in my direction and acted as if
i had gone crazy, *"fuck off!"*

i laughed anxiously as
you pressed your lips into
a grin and asked
"all saying nice things?"

i know they don't
but went ahead and said anyways
"that i can't say for certain."

WHAT I HAVE LEARNED FROM THE DRINKING

boys like to lie
girls like to lie

all i like is
to get high with you.

www.ingramcontent.com/pod-product-compliance
Lightning Source LLC
Chambersburg PA
CBHW032032040426
42449CB00007B/861